W9-CLV-419

BEETLES

NICOLE HELGET

Published by Creative Education
P.O. Box 227, Mankato, Minnesota 56002
Creative Education is an imprint of The Creative Company

Design and production by Stephanie Blumenthal
Printed in the United States of America

Photographs by Guy Bruyea, John Capinera, Whitney Cranshaw, Entomolgical Society of America / Ries Memorial Slide Collection, Getty Images (Robert Harding, Photonica, Taxi, The Image Bank), Dave Leatherman, Frank Peairs

Library of Congress Cataloging-in-Publication Data

Helget, Nicole Lea, 1976–
Beetles / by Nicole Helget.
p. cm. — (BugBooks)
Includes index.
ISBN-13: 978-1-58341-539-9
1. Beetles—Juvenile literature. I. Title.

QL576.2.H45 2007
595.76—dc22   2006018236

First Edition
2 4 6 8 9 7 5 3 1

BEETLES CREEP BY YOUR FEET. THEY CRAWL IN YOUR CARPET. THEY BURROW IN TREES AND DIRT. THEY EAT SMELLY GARBAGE. SOMETIMES THEY LIVE IN THE CORNERS OF YOUR CLOSET. BEETLES ARE EVERYWHERE!

BEETLES ARE INSECTS. THERE ARE MANY DIFFERENT KINDS OF  BEETLES. MANY BEETLES ARE BLACK. BUT BEETLES COME IN LOTS OF COLORS. MOST BEETLES ARE SMALL. BUT SOME ARE AS BIG AS THE PALM OF YOUR HAND!

Beetles come in many colors and sizes.

A BEETLE'S EYES CAN BE LARGE
OR SMALL. BEETLES HAVE STRONG
JAWS. THE JAWS
PINCH AND BITE
FOOD. BEETLES
HAVE TWO FEELERS
ON THEIR HEADS CALLED ANTEN-
NAE (AN-*TEN*-NAY). BEETLES USE
THEM TO SMELL AND TOUCH.

Beetles' jaws are long and sharp.

6

ALL BEETLES HAVE FOUR WINGS AND SIX LEGS. TWO OF THE WINGS ARE HARD. THESE WINGS PROTECT THE BEETLE. THINNER WINGS ARE UNDER THEM. MOST BEE-

TLES DON'T USE THEIR WINGS TO FLY. THEIR BODIES ARE TOO HEAVY.

Most beetles keep their wings folded down.

THE BIGGEST PART OF A BEETLE

IS ITS BELLY. THIS

IS WHERE ITS

FOOD GOES. THE

BELLY ALSO HAS AIR HOLES. THEY

HELP THE BEETLE

BREATHE.

A beetle's belly is long and wide.

DON'T EAT ME! Birds, frogs, and snakes eat beetles. Some beetles squirt predators with liquids that burn or smell bad. This chases the predators away.

A beetle's life begins in an egg. When the egg hatches, a worm comes out. It is called a "larva." The larva eats lots of leaves, grass, or fruit.

Beetle eggs and larvae are small.

THE LARVA'S BODY GROWS TOO BIG FOR ITS SKIN. THE LARVA SHEDS

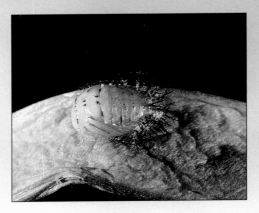

ITS SKIN TO KEEP GROWING. AFTER A WHILE, THE LARVA RESTS. IT HIDES IN THE GROUND OR IN A TREE. THEN IT CHANGES INTO AN ADULT BEETLE.

A larva looks different from an adult beetle.

EGG HIDERS Beetles hide their eggs. The dung beetle
rolls cow droppings into a ball. It lays eggs in the ball.
The oak weevil beetle drills holes in an acorn. It lays its
eggs in the acorn.

ONE OUT OF EVERY FOUR ANI-
MALS IN THE WORLD IS A BEETLE.

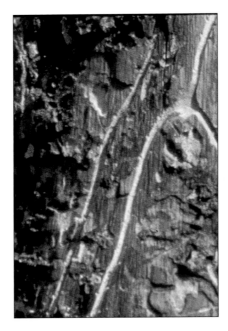

BEETLES LIVE IN DESERTS, FORESTS, AND COLD PLACES. THE ONLY PLACES BEETLES DO NOT LIVE ARE IN THE OCEANS OR AT THE SOUTH POLE.

Beetles can live under tree bark or on leaves.

SOME BEETLES EAT CROPS SUCH
AS POTATOES AND COTTON. THIS
COSTS FARMERS A LOT OF MONEY.
BUT MOST BEETLES ARE HELPFUL.
THEY EAT DEAD ANIMALS AND DEAD

PLANTS. THEY EAT
OTHER BUGS IN GAR-
DENS AND FIELDS, TOO.

Ladybugs eat bugs that chew on leaves.

WORKER BEETLES *Ladybugs are a kind of beetle. Aphids (AF-FIDS) are little bugs that eat crops. Some farmers release ladybugs to keep aphids out of their fields.*

My Pet Beetle   Beetles make good pets. Look under rocks or leaves. If you find a beetle, put it in a box with rocks, wood, and dirt. A piece of lettuce will feed a beetle for weeks.

LOOK AROUND YOUR BACKYARD.

PEEK UNDER ROCKS AND STICKS.

HOW MANY BEETLES CAN YOU FIND?

Beetles can be fun to watch.

BURROW — TO DIG A HOLE OR TUNNEL

CROPS — PLANTS THAT FARMERS GROW

INSECTS — BUGS THAT HAVE SIX LEGS

PREDATORS — ANIMALS THAT KILL AND EAT OTHER ANIMALS

SHEDS — LOSES SKIN

INDEX